Dalwood
Great War Memorial
1914-1919
Our Dalwood Heroes

R. P. Bennett	B. J. Edwards
M. B. Bishop	F. Hoare
J. Davey	E. Hurford
C. Davey	H. Loveridge
M. Davey	F. Pratt
W. Davey	C. R. Parrett
W. L. Driscoll	H. Sweetland
F. Trim	
A. F. Dommett	

Dalwood
Great War Memorial
1914-1919
Our Dalwood Heroes

Alison Morgan

Reveille
PRESS

In
Loving Memory of the
Men of Dalwood
Who died for Home and Freedom
in the Great War
1914 - 1919

For the Fallen

They went with songs to the battle, they were young,
Straight of limb, true of eye, steady and aglow.
They were staunch to the end against odds uncounted;
They fell with their faces to the foe.

They shall grow not old, as we that are left grow old:
Age shall not weary them, nor the years condemn.
At the going down of the sun and in the morning
We will remember them.

Laurence Binyon 1914

Reveille Press is an imprint of
Tommies Guides Military Booksellers & Publishers
PO Box 3229, Eastbourne, East Sussex, BN20 9RZ

www.reveillepress.com

First published in Great Britain by
Reveille Press 2012; Reprinted 2021

For more information please visit
www.reveillepress.com

ISBN 978-1-908336-43-9

Cover design by Reveille Press
Typeset by Graham Hales
Printed and bound in the UK

Contents

Preface

Dalwood is in the east of the County of Devon between the towns of Axminster and Honiton. Until 1844 it was part of the County of Dorset. The earliest recorded Dalwood reference was in a Pipe Roll of 1195 meaning 'dale in the wood'. There are records that it was a Royal Manor. The right to hold an annual fair in Dalwood was granted to William de Chantemerle Lord of the Manor of Dalwood by King Edward III in 1345.

Part One – The Dalwood Men Who Died in the Great War
The Dalwood Great War Memorial of 1914-1919 stands in Dalwood Churchyard in a prominent place in the centre of the village. Sixteen names of the Dalwood men who died in the Great War are inscribed on this. The lives of these men and their families are an important part of Dalwood's history. But what do we know about these men? The surnames and initials are there and the purpose of this book is to throw some light on their lives and their service in the War from the sources available.

Part Two – Dalwood Soldiers' Military Records
There are also fifty one other men associated with Dalwood who served in the Great War and for some of whom military records have been found. These are presented here in Part Two of this book.

There are names listed at the end of this book for whom I have not been able to find any definite records at this time. I continue with this research and welcome any information.

Alison Morgan, Dalwood, October 2012

Part One

Dalwood Men Who Died in The Great War 1914-1919

1. Introduction

Names on the Memorial Cross in Dalwood Churchyard
There are sixteen names inscribed on the Dalwood War Memorial in the Churchyard of St. Peter's Church.

Dalwood parishioners gather every year on 11 November or on Armistice Sunday to remember these men and the many other men from Dalwood and the nation who served in this War. There was great rejoicing when the signing of the Armistice on 11 November 1918 brought the fighting in Europe to an end but at the same time a great sense of loss felt particularly in small communities such as Dalwood where so many local men had lost their lives. Many of these men were buried overseas or in unknown graves in cemeteries overseas. Here was a place where their families could mourn and remember them.

2. Peace Celebrations in 1919

Although the fighting on the Western Front ended on 11 November 1918 the Great War did not end until the signing of the Treaty of Versailles with Germany on 28 June 1919. The people of Dalwood held their own Peace Celebrations on Friday 25 July as reported in *The Western Times* on 1 August 1919:

Dalwood: In glorious weather the Peace celebration took place on Friday afternoon. A hardworking committee of ladies and gentlemen organised and carried through very successfully a varied programme of sports. A free tea was provided for all the parishioners... The people of the parish responded well to a collection a sum of nearly £30 being obtained. Assembling at 2 o'clock in the school playground they marched to a field kindly lent by Mr Cook- farmer at Hutchings Farm. There a united service was held...The children's sports were most successful. The tea was well patronised. A move was then made to a field lent by Mr Philip White in which the adults' sports were held. To complete the day's amusement dancing took place and continued till 11 o'clock. Mr Vincent of Membury brought his swings and big wheel which provided much amusement.

Plans for the Dalwood Memorial

Plans were being made to remember the soldiers who had died. Decisions had to be made as to the form their Memorial should take the choice of a site and the names to be included. In February 1919 Dalwood Parish Council had called a Parish Meeting to consider what steps should be taken in respect of the establishment of a Memorial *To our Brave Boys*. A report of this appeared in *The Western Times* on Friday 11 April 1919:

Dalwood War Memorial: A Committee Meeting was held in the Schoolroom to consider further the proposed erection of a Village Cross as a war memorial Mr W. H. Hoare Secretary B. P. Cox Treasurer. It was decided not to canvass the parish for subscriptions but to ask that donations be sent to the treasurer. The site suggested for the erection of the cross is on ground close to the entrance of the churchyard belonging to Mrs Edwards of Danes Villa. She had kindly promised to give the site on condition that the names only of the fallen be inscribed on the plinth and a book containing the names of all who have served be placed in the church and the chapel.

Subsequently the site chosen for the Dalwood Memorial Cross was on the area which used to be the Village Green now part of the extended churchyard clearly visible on the main road through the village.

1912 St. Peter's Church Dalwood

On 4 July 1919 *The Western Times* reported:

Dalwood: The war memorial is to take the form of a Cross and a tablet is to be affixed in the church and one also in the chapel the cost to be £150. There is every prospect of the amount being raised.

The Western Times on 22 October 1920 carried a report on the Dalwood War Memorial Committee Meeting:

Dalwood A meeting of the War Memorial Committee was held in the Post Office. The secretary presented a balance sheet showing nearly £16 in hand. This will be used to remove a wall and erect iron railings in order to give a better view of the names of the men. Rev. Long congratulated the parishioners on their generous response which means the erection of a lasting memorial to the Dalwood heroes.

The decision to put Memorial Plaques in St. Peter's Church and the Dalwood Methodist Chapel formerly the Bible Christian Chapel recognised the different faiths of the men who died – some as boys had attended the St. Peter's Church Sunday School and worshipped with their families in the Church and some had attended Sunday School at the Dalwood Bible Christian and Methodist Chapel.

In Loving Memory of The Men of Dalwood Who Died for Home and Freedom In the Great War 1914-1919

The names inscribed on the Dalwood Memorial in the Methodist Chapel as seen above were of the men who were born grew up lived and worked in the parish with their families or on the nearby farms and in the area of Ham in the parish of Stockland or had some close family connection with the village.

3. Unveiling the Dalwood Great War Memorial in 1920

The Memorial *To Our Dalwood Heroes of the Great War 1914 to 1919* was unveiled in Dalwood Churchyard in a ceremony on 20 September 1920 led by the Bishop of Exeter. The Dalwood Board School Log Book records the pupils were given a half day's leave to attend this ceremony as described in *The Western Times*:

The Bishop of Exeter unveiled at Dalwood near Axminster yesterday an interior marble tablet and a handsome granite cross in the Churchyard as war memorials. The former bore the inscription: 'In loving memory of the men of Dalwood who died for home and freedom in the Great War 1914-1919' and the latter 'To Our Dalwood heroes' both being inscribed with the names:

R. P. Bennett M. B. Bishop J. Davey C. Davey M. Davey W. Davey W. L. Driscoll B. J. Edwards F. Hoare E. Hurford H. Loveridge F. Pratt C. H. Parrett H. Sweetland F. Trim and A. F. Dommett.

The Vicar the Reverend Long led a service in the church and read the lessons. In an address the Bishop said they had lost sixteen men out of a parish of about 250 and he supposed there were few parishes in England who had suffered more. That memorial was put up as a reminder to those who came after. The country had been saved from a terrible evil by the sacrifice of those who fell in the war but there was a tendency now to speak selfishly. Although the war was over the battle was but half won. There was always a danger after a war. England had need of gallant sons in the war and she had need of unselfish noble-minded people now. Those who remained could not but feel inspired to do their bit as they whom they commemorated did theirs. Sacrifice was admired but not understood here but in the great world beyond sacrifice would be the brilliant the glorious thing. Selfishness pleasure of money-getting would seem like foul and filthy things but sacrifice would be like some glorious resplendent jewel.

1920 Dalwood War Memorial Unveiled Let Unity Prevail
Dalwood sets an example in the movement for a closer union of the churches of all denominations. At the unveiling of the war memorial

tablet in the Dalwood United Methodist Chapel the Pastor Reverend Abbott was supported by the Vicar Reverend Thomas Long while the ceremony was performed by Mrs Ayshford wife of Dr. Ayshford of Dalwood Hill... Western Times 1 October 1920

1920 The War Memorial Unveiled in Dalwood Churchyard

On 11 November 1919 King George V sent a message to the nation for what became an annual Remembrance Celebration:

I believe that my people in every part of the empire fervently wish to perpetuate the memory of that great deliverance and of those who laid down their lives to achieve it. To afford an opportunity for the universal expression of this feeling it is my desire and hope that at the hour when the armistice came into force – the eleventh hour of the eleventh day of the eleventh month – there may be for the brief space of two minutes a complete suspension of all our normal activities. During that time... all work all sound and all locomotion should cease so that in perfect stillness the thoughts of everyone may be concentrated in reverent remembrance of the glorious dead.

Dalwood People have every year continued to make the War Memorial in the Churchyard the focus for their Remembrance of the Dalwood men. Dalwood had a branch of the British Legion for a long time. On Armistice Day War Veterans and the bereaved would march with their medals displayed from Carter's Cross to the War Memorial.

1929 Dalwood United Armistice Service reported in *The Western Times* 15 November 1929

Dalwood – On Sunday a United Armistice Service was held. The Colyton Band gave their services. Between 20 and 30 ex-Service men from Dalwood and Stockland under local resident Colonel Crosbie D.S.O. marched to the village bridge and then to the War Memorial where a United service was held. The wreath was laid by Mrs Hurford Widow of Hawley Bottom. A Sale of poppies realised the sum of over £8.

1935 Dalwood Tribute of Remembrance reported in *The Western Times* Friday 15 November 1935

The annual parade of ex-Service men organised by the local branch of the British Legion took place at Dalwood on Remembrance Sunday. The parade was under the command of Colonel Crosbie D.S.O. President the branch of the Dalwood British Legion and was headed by bugles and drums under the leadership of Mr Wood Colyton. The procession was met at the War Memorial by the Vicar Reverend Butters and the choir...Mrs Peach of Eastons placed the British Legion wreath at the foot of the War Memorial. A collection was taken on behalf of Earl Haig's Fund and amounted to £3 3s. 5d.

Dalwood's Fallen Hero's 1914-1919
by Wallace Azulay

This collage of photos of the men named on the Dalwood War Memorial was made by a local professional photographer Wallace Azulay in 1919 presumably with photos lent by their families. Several are not clearly marked with a name. The ones named are shown with their record.

4. Who Were These Dalwood Men?

The following sources provide some records:

Dalwood Parish Records – The St. Peter's Church Baptism register gives dates for baptism and names of parents. The census returns for the parish of Dalwood every ten years records details of the Dalwood families to which they belonged. The Dalwood Board School Admission Register from 1875 when the school opened gives dates when the pupils were born and admitted to and left the school.

The Commonwealth War Graves Commission 1914-1918 Debt of Honour Register lists the 1.7 million men and women of the Commonwealth forces who died during the two world wars and the 23,000 cemeteries memorials and other locations worldwide where they are *Remembered with Honour*. There is a record available for each person who died which gives brief details of their service.

The Devon Roll of Honour lists all the Devon names.

The UK Soldiers Died in Great War 1914-1918 Register gives some Military Records. These can be found on the website addresses www.ancestry.co.uk. and findmypast.com.

British Army WWI Medal Rolls Index Cards, 1914-1920
This database contains the Medal Rolls Index or Medal Index Cards. These records are not always easily identified and so many have not been found. Every soldier qualified for at least one campaign medal and if he served overseas usually two or three. The three Great War campaign medals were The Star, British War Medal and Victory Medal.

5. The Start of the Great War in 1914

Great Britain declared war on Germany on 4 August 1914. This was in response to Germany's invasion of Belgium. Britain was fulfilling a guarantee also made by France to go to the defence of this small country if it was threatened. The British Army known as The British Expeditionary Force arrived in Belgium and Northern France known from now as the Western Front on 22 August 1914. The first year of the war which began as a war of movement settled into trench warfare by the end of the year. Full Conscription was not introduced until January 1916 but some men were enlisting from the start of the war in 1914 and through 1915 and 1916.

The first Dalwood man recorded as being killed in action was Corporal Edward Hurford on 30 October 1914. As a regular soldier already serving in the army he was with the first British Expeditionary Force to arrive in Northern France. Seven months earlier he had married a local Dalwood girl Sarah Anne Davey of Hawley Bottom at St. Peter's Church. His widow Sarah Hurford remained living in Dalwood for another 48 years. Sarah's youngest brother Private Charles Davey of the Devonshire Regiment was one of the youngest of the men to die at the age of 19 killed in action in Flanders on 6 November 1917.

Two Dalwood men died in the Gallipoli Campaign begun on 25 April 1915 when the Allies landed in what is now the area of Turkey. The second Dalwood man to die was Private Colin Parrett of the Dorsetshire Regiment killed in action on 21 August 1915 in Gallipoli. Private Arthur Dommett of the Dorsetshire Regiment died of his wounds on 1 May 1916 in this campaign.

Private Britton Bishop of the 100th Field Ambulance Royal Army Medical Corps died in Hospital in St. Omer France on 10th January 1916.

Eight other Dalwood men died fighting on the Western Front in France and Flanders. Private Heber Loveridge of the Devonshire Regiment died on 1 July 1916 aged 29 on the first day of the start of the Battle of the Somme with the greatest number of casualties in British military history 60,000. Private Raymond Bennett of the Gloucestershire Regiment the only son of the Dalwood schoolteachers died here two weeks later on 19 July 1916.

Two cousins members of the Davey Family of Hawley Bottom in Dalwood were killed in action on the Western Front. Private John Davey died on 1 February 1916. John Davey had emigrated to Australia in 1913 and returned to fight with the Australian Imperial Forces. Private Walter Davey of the Lancaster Regiment died on 26 September 1917.

Four more Dalwood men died fighting on the Western Front in the last year of the war in Europe. Private Harry Sweetland of the Duke of Cambridge's Own (Middlesex Regiment) died on 21 March 1918. Private Leonard Driscoll of the Duke of Edinburgh's 2nd Battalion Wiltshire Regiment died on 5 June 1918. Private Frederick Trim of the Duke of Edinburgh's Own (Middlesex Regiment) died on 30 August 1918. Private Michael Davey of the Devonshire Regiment was the last of the Dalwood men to die a month before fighting ceased on 8 October 1918.

Two of the Dalwood Soldiers who died in the Great War are buried in Dalwood Churchyard.

Frank Pratt was buried in 1917 - The Dalwood Burial Register records Francis James Pratt aged 25 years of Coombes Head Farm was buried in Dalwood Churchyard on 23 October 1917. He had been discharged from the army as *Unfit for Military Service.*

Three other members of his family were later buried here - Frank Pratt's younger brother William Henry Pratt aged 38 of Lamb Farm was buried 14 December 1936 his mother Harriet Emily aged 75 on 3 June 1949 and father John James Pratt aged 84 on 27 January 1953.

Frederick Hoare's Gravestone is in Dalwood St. Peter's Churchyard under the trees to the left of the Church path. It is a small grey official Commonwealth Gravestone commemorating Lance Corporal Fred Hoare.

Fred Hoare was serving on military service in Exeter Devon when he died of pneumonia on 25 September 1918 at the age of 27. He is included on the Commonwealth Register as being *Remembered* in St. Peter's Churchyard Dalwood as follows.

**In Memory of
Lance Corporal FRED HOARE
51168, 22nd Bn., Welsh Regiment
transf. to (492876), Labour Corps
who died age 27
on 25 September 1918
Son of Mr. and Mrs. W.H. Hoare, of The Poplars,
Dalwood, Kilmington, Devon; husband of Ivy Gladys
Hoare, of The Bungalows, Penslade, Fishguard,
Pembroke.
Remembered with honour
DALWOOD (ST. PETER) CHURCHYARD**

6. The Sixteen Men Named on the Dalwood Memorial

These are recorded here in the order that their name appears on the War Memorial.

Raymond Percy Bennett was born in Dalwood and baptised 5 August 1887 at St. Peter's Church. Raymond was the only son of Edward Bennett and his wife Sarah. His father Edward Bennett was born in 1856 at St. Sidwell's Exeter Devon. After leaving school he trained and was registered as a Teacher. He married Sarah Jane Percy the daughter of James and Sarah Percy at Heavitree Exeter in September 1880.

In April 1881 Edward Bennett Certificated Teacher took up the post of Head Teacher at Dalwood Board School with his wife Sarah as Assistant. The Bennnetts played a leading part in Dalwood life during this period.

Dalwood Board School was opened in April 1875. It was held in a newly enlarged building on the site of the previous old schoolroom built on the edge of St. Peter's Churchyard in 1833 and run as a

1890 Dalwood Board Schoolchildren outside the Old Schoolroom with teachers Mr and Mrs Bennett

Charity or Parochial School. Following the Education Act of 1870 funds were to be made available for schools to be built where the present educational provision was inadequate and new Boards were to be appointed to run these schools. A number of the leading Dalwood parishioners applied for a grant and this school was opened. This building housed a school until 1927 when a new school building outside the village was opened.

The Bennett family lived at what was then known as the School House previously the Old Poor House the thatched cottage opposite the Tucker's Arms now named Old Yew Cottage. They are recorded as the School teachers living here in the census returns for the parish of Dalwood of 1881 1891 1901 and 1911.

Raymond Bennett aged about seven with his Parents outside the School House now Old Yew Cottage

The census return of 1891 records Raymond P. Bennett aged 3 born in Dalwood living at School House in Dalwood Village with his parents Edward aged 35 and Sarah Bennett 37 Schoolmaster and Schoolmistress in Dalwood. Raymond attended Dalwood Board School from 1/3/1892 to 24/10/1902. In the 1901 census return Raymond Bennett was recorded now aged 13 a Scholar living at the School House with his parents Edward aged 45 and Sarah aged 47.

After leaving School in 1902 Raymond was accepted as a pupil teacher trained and worked for Devon County Council. The First

Dalwood School Board Log Book kept by his father the Head Teacher states that in January 1911 Raymond Percy Bennett was helping as a Supply Teacher temporarily in the main room until a new teacher was appointed.

The following entry in the Minute Book of the Dalwood School Board of Managers records this:

1911 May 8 Mr R. Bennett has been asked by the Managers and approved by the County Committee to act as Supply teacher until a permanent teacher be appointed. The School Log Book records June 1911 *Mr R Bennett terminated as Supply Teacher.*

The 1911 census return records Raymond Percy Bennett aged 23 years School Teacher for Devon County Council as a visitor at Wembdon Road Bridgewater Somerset in the household of B. Clench 32 Civil Service P. O. Also staying at this address was Britton John Edwards 28 Bank Clerk born in Dalwood also killed on the Western Front in the Great War.

Raymond Bennett enlisted at Exeter Devon as a Private No. 202343 in the Devonshire Regiment and was later transferred as Private No. 6386 to serve with the Gloucestershire Regiment. There are no more definite records for Raymond until the record of his marriage in March 1916 to Mabel A. Bishop in Tynemouth Northumberland.

Four months later he was killed on 19 July 1916 at the age of 29 in the Battle of Fromelles in France. After a night and a day of fighting 1,500 British and 5,533 Australian soldiers were killed wounded or taken prisoner in this battle.

Private RAYMOND BENNETT No. 6386 of the 2nd/4th Bn. Gloucestershire Regiment formerly No. 202343 Devonshire Regiment was killed at the Battle of Fromelles aged 29 years in France and is Remembered with Honour at Loos Memorial Pas de Calais France. Husband of M. A. Bennett of The Nest Overmoigne Dorchester Dorset. The Loos Memorial commemorates over 20,000 officers and men who have no known grave.

Maurice Britton Bishop was born 31 March 1896 in Dalwood. Maurice was the youngest son of George and Anna Bishop. His father was born in Northleigh and his mother born in Dalwood they had a total of 13 children but six died in childhood. His parents were members of the Dalwood Bible Christian Chapel later known as the United Methodist Chapel. He was baptised at the Dalwood Bible Christian Chapel on 3 April 1896. He attended Dalwood Bible Christian later the Methodist Sunday School in years 1902-1906 and 1908-1912.

In 1901 the family was living in Andrewshayes Lane Dickens Marsh – his father George was employed as a Farm Carter age 51 at Andrewshayes Farm and his mother Anna aged 49 Nancy 60 from Henstridge who was his widowed aunt and was blind and an elder brother William 14 and elder sister Daisy 11 both born in Dalwood. Maurice B. Bishop was aged 5.

Britton Bishop attended Dalwood Board School from 7/5/1901 to 10/5/1910. In 1911 Maurice's parents still lived in Andrewshayes Lane with son William now 24 a Farm Labourer and daughter Daisy 21 working at home . His father now 61 was a Farm Carter and his mother now 59 and an invalid was being cared for by Daisy. Meanwhile Maurice now aged 15 years was living and working for Farmer James Sprague at Haddon Farm in Wilmington Devon.

Military Records show that Britton Bishop Farm Labourer enlisted for the Duration of the War at the age of 19 years 5 months at Axminster Devon on 7 September 1915. Private Britton Bishop No. 66441 embarked with his Field Ambulance Unit from Southampton on 17/11/1915 and landed at Le Havre in France on 18/11/1915 to serve with the BEF. He died about thirty days later in hospital at St. Omer which was the General Headquarters of the British Expeditionary Force from October 1914 to March 1916.

Private BRITTON BISHOP No. 66441 of the 100th Field Ambulance Royal Army Medical Corps died on 10th January 1916 aged 19 of Celebral Spinal Meningitis in No. 7 General Hospital St.Omer Northern France. Son of George and Anna Bishop of Dickens Marsh Dalwood Devon. He is Remembered with Honour at Longuenesse Souvenir Cemetery St. Omer France.

Longuenesse Souvenir Cemetery St. Omer France

About The Davey Family of Hawley Bottom Dalwood in the Great War

There are four Davey names inscribed on the Dalwood Great War Memorial. All four fought and died on the Western Front in France and Flanders.

John Davey died in 1916 aged 25
Charles Davey died in 1917 aged 19
Walter Davey died in 1917 aged 35
Michael Davey died in 1918 aged 22 years

Three – John, Walter and Michael – were first cousins whose grandparents John and Sarah Davey came from the parish of Widworthy Devon to live and work in the parish of Dalwood in 1842.

Charles Davey was not closely related although he lived nearby – his father James was the son of William and Sarah Davey of Stockland who came to live in Hawley Bottom Dalwood near the three other Davey families.

A number of other members of this Davey family served in the Great War. There are details for these in Part Two of this book.

John Davey was born 20 June 1891 in Dalwood and baptised at St. Peter's Church on 16 August 1891.

His parents were Thomas and Hannah Davey of Hawley Bottom Dalwood who lived near to the families of his two cousins Michael and Walter Davey who also died in the Great War.

John Davey attended Dalwood Board School from 4/5/1896 to 30/5/1905 and the Dalwood Bible Christian Sunday School 1902-1905. In 1901 John Davey aged 9 was living in a cottage at Hawley Bottom next to Larkshayes Farm with his family. His father Thomas 54 was employed as a Groom and Gardener his mother Hannah was 46 and he had five brothers George 24 a Railway Plate Layer

Walter 22 a Miller's Labourer Tom 18 a Coach builder and two younger brothers Fred 5 and Arthur 3 and two sisters Annie 12 and Euphemia 6 all born and baptised in Dalwood.

By the time of the next census in 1911 John Davey aged 19 was now trained as a Wheelwright Journeyman working at Cad Green Ilton Ilminster in Somerset and living with his uncle Richard Hayman 58 who was a Wheelwright & Carpenter and aunt Mary aged 48 and two other members of his Davey family – John's elder sister Bessie Hayman Davey 26 a Shirt Machinist born in Dalwood and younger brother Fred Davey 15 born in Dalwood who was learning the Wheelwright business.

In 1914 John Davey aged 23 years is recorded on the Ships Passenger Lists emigrating to Australia arriving at Brisbane Queensland on the *Orsova* on 20 July 1914. After becoming an Australian national he enlisted on 1 September 1915 in the Australian Imperial Forces at Toowoomba in the State of Queensland. John Davey died within four months of arriving in France.

John Davey Private No. 3796 9/26th Battalion Australian Imperial Forces

Detailed records of his Enlistment Service Casualty and Missing in Action Records can be found in the Australian National Archives as follows:

31/1/1916 Embarked at Brisbane per H. M. A. T *'Vandalla'.*

2/4/1916 Allotted to and proceeded to join 50th Battalion in France.

2/4/1916 Transferred from 26th En. To 52nd Battalion 13th Infantry AIF.

15/8/1916 Reported Missing in Action in France.

4/9/1916 Confirmed as Missing Killed in Action.

Private JOHN DAVEY No. 3796 52nd Battalion Australian Infantry AIF died aged 25 on 4 September 1916 on the Western Front. He is Remembered with Honour at Villers-Bretonneux Memorial east of Amiens France. Son of Thomas and Hannah Davey of Hawley Bottom Dalwood Devon later of the United States of America.

Charles Davey was born on 13 August 1898 in Dalwood and baptised on 2 October 1898 at St. Peter's Church. He was the youngest of eight children of James and Mary Ann Davey. His father James Davey was baptised at St. Peter's Church Dalwood on 1 January 1854 son of William and Sarah Labourer of Stockland Devon.

Charles Davey's family is recorded in the census returns for Dalwood living at Battle Cottage in Hawley Bottom near the other three Davey families in the area whose children died in the Great War but they were not related.

In 1901 Charles Davey aged 2 was living at Battle Cottage in Hawley Bottom with his father James 47 who was an Agricultural labourer his mother Mary 45 and five sisters Sarah Jane 15 Florence 12 Elizabeth 9 Ida 7 and Susan 4. Charlie Davey attended Dalwood Board School from 25/4/1904 to 12/8/1912 when he left to work with his father.

His two elder brothers William and John fought in the Great War. In 1902 John Davey Charles' elder brother enlisted in the Army and served throughout the War.

In 1911 the family address was still Battle Cottage and Charles was aged 12 and a scholar at Dalwood School. He was living with his father James 58 Farm labourer and mother Mary 56 brother William 28 a Farm labourer and sisters Sarah Jane 25 and Susan 15 who both now worked as Brush drawers fixing bristles into the handles of brushes.

As previously recorded three years later on 6 March 1914 Charles' elder sister Sarah Jane Davey married Edward Hurford at St. Peter's Church Dalwood. Edward Hurford was killed in action on 30 October 1914 aged 29 just six months after his marriage. His name is also inscribed on the Dalwood Memorial.

Charles Davey's mother Mary Anne Davey of Hawley Bottom died aged 62 and was buried on 12 January 1917 in Dalwood Churchyard.

Private CHARLES DAVEY No. 65346 of the 1st Battalion Devonshire Regiment was killed in action on 6 November

1917 aged 19 on the Western Front. He is Remembered with Honour at the Memorial at Tyne Cot Belgium.

The Tyne Cot Memorial to the Missing commemorates 34,887 names of men from the United Kingdom and New Zealand Forces who died from the date of 16th August 1917 and who have no known grave.

Tyne Cot Cemetery Belgium

Michael Emanuel Davey was born in Dalwood on 24 December 1895 and baptised 19 January 1896 at St. Peter's Church.

Michael was a cousin of John and Walter Davey whose names are also inscribed on the War Memorial. Michael's father was Emanuel Davey born in 1851 the youngest son of John and Sarah Davey.

Michael attended Dalwood Board School from 29/4/1901 to 23/9/1909. He also attended the Dalwood Bible Christian Sunday School.

In 1901 Michael Davey aged 5 was living at an unnamed cottage in Hawley Bottom with his father Emanuel aged 49 employed as a Railway Plate Layer on the nearby London and South Western Railway route from Yeovil to Exeter opened in 1860 which passed through the parish of Dalwood. His mother was Mary then 42 born in Whitford and brothers and sisters George 8 Robert 6 Michael 5 Mabel 3 and Eva aged 11 months all born in Dalwood. In 1911 Michael Davey now aged 15 was one of two Servants living  with and employed as a Cow Boy for farmer Robert Banks and his family at Hamberhayne Farm Colyton Devon. On 28 April 1915 Michael Davey commenced military service in France.

Private MICHAEL EMANUEL DAVEY No.9890 Devonshire Regiment 9th Service Battalion was killed in action aged 22 on 8 October 1918 on the Western Front in the last month of fighting here before the Armistice of 11 November 1918. He is Remembered with Honour at the Memorial Vis-En Artois Pas de Calais France & Flanders.

Michael Davey was awarded Three Medals for his service in France – The Star, British War and Victory Medals.

The Vis-en-Artois Cemetery accommodates the remains of 2,369 soldiers of whom 885 have been identified. These soldiers had been taking part in the last offensive against the Germans in this area of France which ended the war.

Walter Albion Davey was born on 2 August 1882 and baptised on 20 August 1882 at St. Peter's Church Dalwood. Walter was the first cousin of John and Michael Davey named on the Dalwood War Memorial born and also living in Hawley Bottom Dalwood. Walter was the youngest son of Albion and Sarah Anne Davey of Hawley Bottom Dalwood. Albion Davey was the third of John and Sarah Davey's children the first to be baptised at St. Peter's Church Dalwood on 25 July 1841. Walter attended Dalwood Board School from 16/4/1888 to 30/3/1894.

In 1891 Walter was aged 8 and living at Hawley Bottom Dalwood with his father Albion 49 who was employed as a Horse Carter on a Farm his mother Sarah 50 who was working as a Laundress two elder brothers John 21 a Shoemaker and James 12 and his maternal grandmother Sarah Wood 79 widow.

The 1901 census records Walter aged 19 was employed as a miner in Wales working as a Coal Hewer and boarding with the Young family at 15 Hillside Ystradyfodwg Glamorgan in Wales.

In 1911 Walter was now employed as a Labourer and was back living at Hawley Bottom in a three room cottage with his parents Albion Davey 70 who was the Dalwood Sexton and general labourer, and Sarah Anne 72 and their grandson Alfred Pester 12 who was attending school.

Walter's father Albion Davey died suddenly aged 71 years and was buried in Dalwood Churchyard on 8 August 1912. He was the Church Sexton and the leading Bell Ringer. His sudden death was recorded in *The Western Times* Friday 9 August 1912:

DALWOOD on Sunday evening, after ringing what described as good peal, the Sexton of Dalwood Devon Mr. Albion Davey sat down in the nearest pew and suddenly expired. This caused such consternation that the curate-in-charge Rev. Roberts immediately postponed the service. A ringer for nearly 50 years Albion will be greatly missed by those whom he trained to ring. The churchyard over which he took such care has looked of late quite a quiet peaceful resting place. The jury of whom Mr Philip White of Brooks Cottage was chosen foreman after hearing the evidence of Mr Walter Davey son of the deceased and Mr Job Summers who was ringing with him at the time returned a verdict in accordance with the medical evidence that deceased died of Heart failure. The jury gave their fees to the widow.

Walter's elder brother James born in 1879 also served in the army during the Great War. He had enlisted in the army in 1904 and served throughout the War.

Private WALTER ALBION DAVEY No. 30513 of the 8th Battalion King's Own Royal Lancaster Regiment age 35 was killed in action on 26 September 1917 at Zonnebeke on the Western Front in France and Flanders. Son of Albion and Sarah Anne Davey of Hawley Bottom Dalwood Devon. He is Remembered with Honour at Tyne Cot Memorial to the Missing in Belgian Flanders.

Walter Davey was awarded the British War and Victory Medals.

Walter Leonard Driscoll was born in Dalwood on 18 May 1899 the son of William and Elizabeth Jane Driscoll. He was baptised on 23 July 1899 at St. Peter's Church Dalwood. In 1901 the family was living at Slate House at the top of Danes Hill – now Thorny Cleave. His father William born in Somerset was then 32 and working as a General Farm labourer his mother Elizabeth 27 was born in Yarcombe. He had an elder sister Elizabeth aged 3 born in Membury.

Leonard Driscoll attended Dalwood Board School from 25/4/1904 to 19/5/1913. In 1911 the family was living at Cuckolds Pit (variation Cuckoos Pit) in the parish of Stockland – a group of cottages over the top of Danes Hill on the path down to the River Yarty.

His father William Driscoll 43 was employed as a Mason's Labourer and he now had three sisters – Elizabeth 13 Lilian 9 and Winifred 3 months born in Dalwood and one brother Lionel born in Stockland.

Leonard Driscoll enlisted at Exeter Devon as Private No. 35262 in the Duke of Edinburgh's 2nd Battalion Wiltshire Regiment.

Private LEONARD DRISCOLL No. 35262 The Duke of Edinburgh's 2nd Battalion Wiltshire Regiment was killed in action on 5 June 1918 age 19 years on the Western Front in France and Flanders in the last months of the war. He is Remembered with Honour at Soissons Memorial France. Son of William and Elizabeth Driscoll of Cuckoo's Pit Stockland Devon.

The Soissons Memorial commemorates almost 4,000 officers and men of the United Kingdom forces who died during the Battles of the Aisne and the Marne in 1918 and who have no known grave.

Britton John Edwards was born on 3 February 1883 in Dalwood the third son of William Edwards Junior Dealer and Shopkeeper and Mary Anne Edwards. He was baptised at St. Peter's Church on 3 May 1883.

At least three generations of the Edwards family lived in the parish of Dalwood and kept the Shop and Post Office in the centre of the Village – James Edwards 1762-1852 his son William Edwards Senior 1813 – 1897 and his son William Edwards Junior 1838 – 1912. Over many years they acquired farms cottages and lands in the parish of Dalwood and the surrounding area.

In June 1877 William Edwards Junior married Mary A. Dymond of Axminster. They had seven children baptised at St. Peter's Church: Arthur James 9 April 1878 William 11 February 1880 Britton John 3 May 1883 Ernest 19 September 1884 Victor Harry 7 December 1886 Ellen Maude 8 February 1889 and Allan Dymond born 1895. Three of their sons served in the Great War.

Britton John Edwards attended Dalwood Board School from 9/4/1888 to 3/8/1896. In 1891 Britton aged 8 and his elder brother William Edwards aged 11 were living with their grandfather in the parish of Stockland John Dymond 68 a Widower Farmer born in Offwell and Eliza White his sister in law and Housekeeper.

At this time in 1891 his parents were living in Dalwood Village at the Village Shop and House called 'Lakes'. William Edwards 53 was the Grocer and Dealer and his wife Mary Ann 38 together with their other children Arthur James 13 Victor Harry 4 and Ellen Maud 2 who were all born in Dalwood. They had a domestic servant Ellen Hoyel living with them. In 1901 the family had moved to live at Danes Villa at the top of Danes Hill – William aged 63 Retired Grocer 63 and Mary 47 with sons William 21 Victor 14 Ellen 12 and Allan Dymond aged 6.

In 1901 Britton Edwards was an 18 year old working as a Bank Clerk and was a Boarder living with Emma Eveleigh 61 in Camden Road Bridgwater Somerset. In April 1911 Britton now aged 28 was still employed as a Bank Clerk and was staying as one of two visitors with the Cleach family at 55 Wemdon Road Bridgewater Somerset – the other visitor staying was Raymond Bennett 23 School Teacher also of Dalwood and who is also remembered on the Dalwood War Memorial.

Britton Edward's father William died and was buried on the 13 May 1912 in Dalwood Churchyard. Two of Britton's younger brothers Victor Harry and Allan Dymond Edwards also enlisted and served in this war.

Britton John Edwards living at Teignmouth enlisted at Newton Abbott Devon as Private No. 66836 in the Devonshire Regiment.

Private BRITTON JOHN EDWARDS No. 66836 of the Devonshire Regiment 2nd Battalion aged 35 was killed in action in the last months of the war on 27 May 1918 in France & Flanders. He is Remembered with Honour at Soissons Memorial Aisne France.

This commemorates almost 4,000 officers and men of the United Kingdom forces who died during the Battles of the Aisne and the Marne in 1918 and who have no known grave.

News that Britton John Edwards had been killed in action in 1918 was reported in the local paper *The Western Times* on 5 July 1918: *News has been officially received that Private B. J. Edwards of the Devons is missing in France. He is the son of the late Mr W. Edwards and of Mrs Edwards of Danes Villa Dalwood. He was previous to his enlistment cashier in Lloyds Bank at Teignmouth. Mrs Edwards has two other sons serving one of whom Private V. H. Edwards is in hospital suffering from a compound fracture of the left arm. He was in Canada at the outbreak of the war and came over with the 5th Canadians. This is the third time he has been wounded. The other son is Trooper Allan D. Edwards who is serving in Palestine.*

Frederick Hoare was born in the parish of Membury Devon in 1890. Fred was the eldest child of William Henry Hoare who was a Bootmaker and Farmer and Ellen Hoare. In 1891 Fred aged one year was living with his parents at Mount Pleasant Membury William H. Hoare 31 Boot and Shoemaker Ellen 36 both born in Dalwood. By 1896 the family had moved to the parish of Dalwood when Fred was admitted to Dalwood Board School 27/10/1896 which he left on 10/3/1904.

Three generations of the Hoare family lived and worked in the parish of Dalwood as Bootmakers and leaders of the Bible Christian and Methodist community. Fred's grandfather James Hoare was a founder of the Bible Christian Chapel in Dalwood in 1868. His father William Henry Bootmaker and Farmer was Assistant Overseer for the Parish Council and the Correspondent/ Clerk of Dalwood School for forty years. Fred and his sisters attended the Dalwood Bible Christian Sunday School.

In 1901 Fred was aged 11 living at The Shrubbery Dalwood between Laurel Cottage and The Rising Sun with his parents William H Hoare 41 Boot Manufacturer and Farmer with 12 acres of land and Ellen 46 and three younger sisters Lilly 7 Alma 4 born Membury and Dora 2 born Dalwood. Living with them was George Abbott 25 Journeyman Bootmaker born Wambrook Somerset who later became the Methodist Pastor in Dalwood.

In 1911 Fred Hoare now 21 a Boot and Shoe maker was still living with his family at Rising Sun Farm now known as Poplars. His father William Henry Hoare was 51 also a Boot Shoemaker and Farmer Ellen 56 and sisters Lily 17 Alma 14 Dora 12 with a Boarder named Sims Clapp 31 a Methodist Minister.

After January 1916 when conscription made enlistment compulsory Fred Hoare was one of a number of Dalwood men who came before the Devon War Tribunals at Axminster Court on appeal as reported in the local paper: *Fred Hoare 25 single boot maker and repairer of Dalwood appealed against the decision of the local tribunal who refused him exemption. In part time he attended cattle for his father. The reason for the refusal was that the father could superintend the business but the appellant said this was impossible due to his father's ill health. Personally he was very willing to go and he placed himself entirely in the hands of the Tribunal. In confirming the decision of the local tribunal the Chairman said they appreciated the spirit shown by the appellant.*

Fred Hoare Private No. 51168 enlisted with the 22nd Welsh Regiment on 11 May 1916 at Axminster Devon. He was later transferred as Private No. 492876 to the Labour Corps where he acted as a Clerk in the Military Office Exeter Devon and was promoted to Lance Corporal.

On 28 July 1917 Fred Hoare married Ivy Gladys Wareham at the Wesleyan Chapel in Newton Abbott Devon – she had been the Infants' teacher at Dalwood Board School from 1911 to 1913. They had a daughter Phyllis Edna born 25 April 1918 and baptised on 2 June 1918 at the Dalwood Methodist Chapel.

The Hoare Family in the Garden at Poplars

1917 Fred Hoare's Wedding to Ivy Gladys Wareham

Private FRED HOARE No. 51168 22nd Battalion Welsh Regiment transferred to No. 492876 Labour Corps promoted Lance Corporal died of pneumonia contracted on 25 September 1918 on military duty age 27 at No. 2 Military Hospital Exeter. Son of William Henry and Ellen Hoare of Poplars Dalwood Devon.

Fred Hoare was buried in Dalwood Churchyard on 30 September 1918 the service taken by Pastor George Abbott. His gravestone is maintained by the War Grave Commission. Fred's widow Ivy Gladys Hoare died in 1970. Her name is inscribed on his gravestone. His daughter died in 1994.

There is a separate plaque remembering Fred Hoare in the Dalwood Methodist Chapel of which he and his family were members. Fred Hoare is also remembered on the Fishguards War Memorial in Wales the home of his widow.

Edward Hurford was born in 1885 at Cooks Moor in the parish of Upottery Devon. He was the youngest child of Clement Hurford an Agricultural Labourer and his wife Ann. In 1891 Edward aged 6 was living with his family at Cooks Moor Upottery. His father Clement Hurford age 49 was born in Monkton and employed as a Labourer his mother Ann age 49 was born in Clayhidon and he had two elder brothers Robert 25 and John 10. In 1901 Edward Hurford now aged 16 was living and working as a Carter on a farm for Farmer John Melhuish 74 at Claypitts Farm in the parish of Upottery.

1902 Military Records of Attestation for Edward Hurford
Edward Hurford enlisted in the army on 21 August 1902 at Chard Somerset aged 18 years and 4 months as a Private No. 45432 in the 4th Devons – Edward Hurford of Cooks Moor in the parish of Upottery Honiton Devon now residing in Stockland Employer George White Age 18 years and 4 months working as a Labourer Single. He gave his next of kin as his parents Clement and Ann Hurford of Cooksmoor Cottage Upottery Devon. Signed Edward Hurford Record of Oath taken.

Description given – Height 5 ft 3" Weight 128 pounds Chest 35" Fair blue eyes light colour hair Church of England.

Certificate of Medical Examination – *I consider him fit for the Militia Signed Medical Recruiting Officer 21 August 1902 in Chard Somerset.*

1904 28 May Private Edward Hurford transferred from the Devon 4th to the 3rd Battalion Somerset Light Infantry now Private No. 4532 in the 3rd Battalion the Somerset Light Infantry.

1911 The census returns for 1911 record his name in the Overseas Military Return of Men Serving in the Army as Edward Hurford Lance Corporal aged 26 born Cooks Moor Honiton Devon.

1914 Edward Hurford aged 29 married Sarah Jane Davey aged 28 of Hawley Bottom Dalwood on 6 March 1914 at St. Peter's Church Dalwood.

Sarah Jane Davey was the eldest daughter of James and Sarah Jane Davey of Battle Cottage now Honeysuckle Cottage Hawley Bottom. She was born on 21 January 1886 and baptised on 21 February 1886 at St. Peter's Church Dalwood. In 1901 she was living with her family at Battle Cottage in Hawley Bottom with her father James 47 Agricultural labourer and mother Mary Anne 44 and Florence 12 Elizabeth 9 Ida 7 Susan 4 and only brother Charles aged 2 years all born in Dalwood – Sarah Jane aged 15 was recorded as working at home as a Brush Maker Hair and Tooth.

In 1911 the address of the family was still Battle Cottage Sarah Jane now 25 a Brush Drawer with her parents James 58 Farm Labourer Mary Anne 56 brother William 28 Farm Labourer Sister Susan 15 also a Brush Drawer and Charles aged 12 at school. Sarah Jane Davey attended Dalwood Board School from 1/6/1891 to 20/5/1898.

Her husband Edward Hurford was killed in action in Northern France in the early days of the war on 30 October 1914 eight months after the marriage. Sarah Jane's youngest brother Charles Davey was also killed in the war in 1917. After her husband was killed in action Sarah Jane Hurford continued to live at Battle Cottage in Hawley Bottom until her death in June 1963 and she is buried in St. Peter's Churchyard. She was the last surviving member of the Davey Family in Hawley Bottom.

Corporal EDWARD HURFORD No. 9002 King's Own Yorkshire Light Infantry 2nd Battalion age 29 was killed in action on 30 October 1914 in Northern France. Edward Hurford is Remembered with Honour at the Le Touret Memorial France.

The Memorial in Le Touret Military Cemetery Richebourg-l'Avoue is one of those erected by the Commonwealth War Graves Commission to record the names of the officers and men who fell in the Great War and whose graves are not known. It covers the period from the arrival of the II Corps in Flanders in 1914 to the eve of the Battle of Loos and commemorates over 13,000 servicemen who fell in this area before 25 September 1915 and who have no known grave.

Edward Hurford was awarded three Medals – The Star, British War and Victory Medals.

Le Touret Military Cemetery

Heber Loveridge was born on 2 October 1887 in Ham in the parish of Stockland. He attended Dalwood Board School from 4/4/1892 to 28/3/1902. His parents were John and Catherine Loveridge. His father John born in 1842 in Stockland was a Blacksmith who married Catherine Glade youngest daughter of Samuel and Charlotte Glade of Yarcombe Devon on 28 November 1865 at St. Peter's Church Dalwood. They had a Smithy and Shop at Ham.

The 1881 census return records the family was living in Ham Stockland at the Smith Shop John Loveridge 38 Blacksmith Caroline 37 born Upottery and children Harry 15 Albert 13 Willie 13 Tom 10 Minnie 7 Fred 5 and Jesse aged 3 all born in Stockland with his mother Martha 72 a Nurse born in Combpyne.

In 1891 Heber Loveridge aged 3 was living at Myrtle Cottage in Ham with his father John aged 48 a Blacksmith and mother Catherine 47 and his elder brothers and sisters Tom 18 a Miller's Assistant and sisters Minnie 17 Jesse 13 and Laura 6 all born in Ham Stockland. In 1901 Heber Loveridge now aged 13 at school was still living with his family in Ham – his father John Loveridge

Houses in Ham Stockland

The Old Shop Ham Stockland kept by Minnie Loveridge

58 Corn Dealer and Blacksmith mother Catherine 57 elder brother Fred Loveridge aged 25 Civil Servant Post Office Sorting Clerk and sister Laura 16.

In 1911 Heber Loveridge aged 22 was a Grocer's Assistant boarding with the Banger family William Short Banger aged 44 a Life Assurance Agent and Emily at Cheapside Langport Somerset.

Private HEBER LOVERIDGE No. 20601 of the 2nd Battalion Devonshire Regiment was killed in action on 1 July 1916 age 29 on the first day of the Battle of the Somme in Northern France.

It was noted that: *July 1st 1916. This particular day had an extremely high casualty rate – 57,470 British casualties including 19,240 men killed. Very hazy but the mist lifted at 7.30 a.m. when the Allied attack began. The offensive was a combined Franco-British one on a 25-mile front both north and south of the Somme... Thirteen divisions of Commonwealth forces supported by a French attack to the south launched an offensive on a line from north of Gommecourt to Maricourt. Despite a preliminary bombardment lasting seven days, the German defences were barely touched and the attack met unexpectedly fierce resistance. Losses were catastrophic and with only minimal advances on the southern flank the initial attack was a failure.*

Heber Loveridge is Remembered with Honour at the Thiepval Memorial in France with no known grave.

This was the Memorial to the Missing of the Somme bearing the names of more than 72,000 officers and men of the United Kingdom and South African forces who died in the Somme sector before 20 March 1918 and have no known grave. Over 90% of those commemorated died between July and November 1916. It was opened on 31 July 1932 by the Prince of Wales and remains the largest British war memorial in the world. 150ft high and dominating the surrounding area the memorial was designed by Sir Edwin Lutyens.

Thiepval Memorial France

Francis James Pratt known as Frank was born in August 1892 in the parish of Offwell Devon.

He was the eldest child of William and Emily Pratt. In 1901 aged 9 Francis was living with his family at Burrowhayes in the parish of Colyton Devon. His father William J. 32 born in Ottery St. Mary was employed as an Agricultural Labourer and his mother Emily 27 was born in Northleigh. He had a younger sister Florence 7 born Southleigh and brother William 4 born  Colyton. In 1911 the family was now living in a four room cottage at Lower Hawley Dalwood and Frank aged 19 was employed as a General Labourer. His younger brother William was now 14 and his younger sister Florence 17 was living elsewhere.

Military Records Proceedings of Discharge Casualty Form for Frank Pratt

Frank Pratt enlisted on 12 September 1914 and served for three years as Private No. 19078 in the Grenadier Guards 5th Battalion. His trade was a Groom. He served in France & Flanders from 15 August 1915 to 6 August 1917 when he became seriously ill. He was transferred to London and discharged on 13 September 1917 at the age of 25 as *no longer physically fit for War Service due to Pulmonary Tuberculosis.* He had served three years and two days. He was returned to his family at the address Coombs Head Farm Dalwood. His Military Character was described as *Very Good Clean Sober and Hardworking.*

Private FRANK PRATT No. 19078 of the 4th Battalion Grenadier Guards was discharged from the army on 13 September 1917. Frank Pratt died on 19 October 1917 age 25 years and was buried on 23 October 1917 in St. Peter's Churchyard Dalwood.

Frank Pratt was awarded The British War and Victory Medals.

Colin Rupert Symons Parrett was born in 1895 in the parish of Membury Devon.

In 1891 Colin's parents were living at South Devon Place in Plymouth Devon – his father Thomas Benjamin Parrett born in Whitford Devon aged 24 was living on his own means and married to Zoe 24 who was born in New York.

In 1901 Colin Parrett aged 6 years was living at Western Cottage Kilmington with his parents Thomas 34 a Seedsman's Agent and wife Zoe Parrett 34 a New York British Subject and his elder brother Leslie 10 born in Plymouth. In 1911 Colin Parrett aged 16 was employed as an Assistant Worker on a farm living and working with the family of Farmer Arthur White and his wife Lily at Dalwood Hill Farm in the parish of Dalwood. Colin's parents Thomas Parrett 44 a Seedsman's Agent and Zoe 44 were now living at Millwater Cottage in Dalwood.

Colin Parrett of "D" Company 5th Dorsetshire Regiment arrived for Service in the Balkans on 11 July 1915. A month later he was killed in action.

Private COLIN RUPERT SYMONS PARRETT No. 10027 of "D" Company 5th Dorsetshire Regiment aged 20 killed in action on 21 August 1915 during the assault on Turkish trenches between Aire Kayak and Susak Kuyu Suvla in Gallipoli in the Balkans . He is Remembered with Honour at the Helles Memorial Turkey Gallipoli.

Colin Parrett was awarded The Star, British War and Victory Medals. Colin's elder brother Leslie Parrett also enlisted and entered the campaign in France on 30 June 1915. Their father Thomas Parrett served as a Churchwarden at St. Peter's Church Dalwood from 1918 to 1936. He died 24 November 1936 aged 69 and was buried on 28 November in St. Peter's Churchyard. His gravestone can be seen by the West door of the Church.

Harry Sweetland was born 25 May 1881 in Dalwood.

He was baptised on 7 August 1881 at St. Peter's Church and he attended Dalwood Board School from 5/4/1886 to 26/3/1894. Harry was the third of eight children born to Joseph William and Sarah Jane Sweetland of Evenses Cottage on Danes Hill Dalwood. His father Joseph William Sweetland aged 21 Mason had married Sarah Jane Newton on 16 April 1874 at St. Peter's Church Dalwood. Sarah Jane was baptised 8 January 1854 at St. Peter's Church the daughter of Thomas Newton farmer. In 1861 Thomas Newton 42 born in Kilmington was the Innkeeper and Farmer of 21 acres at Bagaton Old Inn with wife Ann 41 Isabella Ann 12 Elizabeth Mary 9 Sarah Jane 7 Eliza 4 born in Stockland.

In 1891 Harry Sweetland was living with his family at an unnamed cottage on Dennis Hill Dalwood – Joseph W Sweetland 38 a Mason born Somerset Sarah Jane 37 born in Dalwood William 16 Henry 10 Ada 7 Frederick 5 Herbert 4 Elsie 1 all born in Dalwood. Ten years later in 1901 Harry was still living with his parents Joseph William & Sarah Jane Sweetland at Evenses Danes Hill Dalwood. Harry was aged 13 and employed as a Grocer's assistant and his father was still a Mason.

In 1911 Harry's family was again listed as living at Evenses a four room cottage in Dalwood his father now 58 a self-employed House Builder Sarah Anne 57 with daughter Gladys 15. Joseph and Sarah had ten children born in Dalwood three of whom had died.

Their son Harry Sweetland has not been found in this 1911 census.

Private HENRY HARRY SWEETLAND No. 32398 of the 23rd Battalion Duke of Cambridge's Own (Middlesex Regiment) was killed in action on 21 March 1918 aged 37

years on the Western Front in France and Flanders. Son of Joseph and Sarah Sweetland of Evenses Dalwood Devon. He is Remembered with Honour at Red Cross Corner Cemetery Beugny France.

Casualty Details given for this Memorial in France are: UK 205 Australia 10 South Africa 4 Germany 1 Total Burials: 220.

Harry Sweetland was awarded the Victory Medal.

Red Cross Corner Cemetery Beugny France

Frederick Trim was born in 1895 in the parish of Shute Devon. He was the eldest child of George and Ellen Trim of Holmes Knapp Dalwood. Frederick's grandfather George Trim had come to the parish of Dalwood about 1880 with his wife Maria from Musbury Devon. In 1891 George was the Innkeeper at the Carpenters Arms one of several Inns in Dalwood which have now disappeared. There is now a house there named Carpenters. His son George born 1872 was working as a Carpenter living with the family.

In 1901 George Trim 29 Carpenter was living at Holmes Knapp in Dalwood with wife Ellen 28 born in Stockland and children Harry 4 and Charlie 2 and twins Leonard and Ida one month old all born in Dalwood. Their son Frederick Trim was aged 6 and was living with his grandparents in the village and parish of Stockland. His grandfather Henry Newton was aged 56 employed as an Agricultural Labourer with his wife Mary and son Albert 26 a Shoemaker.

In 1911 Frederick Trim aged 16 working as a Wheelwright and Carpenter was living at Cox Hill Churchstanton in Somerset with his uncle James Berry aged 29 who was a Wheelwright and Carpenter and his wife Emily 32 who was born in Stockland and their two year old son William Henry.

In 1911 Frederick's parents were still living at Holmes Knapp in Dalwood his father George 39 was a Journeyman Carpenter and they were living with their seven other children Charlie 12 Apprentice Carpenter Laura 10 Leonard Trim Gladys 4 Hilda 4 born in Dalwood.

Frederick Trim enlisted at Taunton Somerset with the Cambridge's Own (Middlesex Regiment). He entered the campaign in France on 23 August 1915. His younger brother Edward Trim also fought in the Great War. Edward Trim enlisted on 13 July 1916.

Frederick Trim's name appears on the Stockland Memorial as well as the Dalwood Memorial.

Private FREDERICK TRIM No. 202409 of the 1st/7th Battalion Duke of Cambridge's Own (Middlesex Regiment) was killed in action on 30 August 1918 aged 22 years in the last phase of fighting the war in France and Flanders. Son of George and Ellen Trim of Holmes Knapp Dalwood Devon. Frederick Trim is Remembered with Honour at Vis-En-Artois Memorial in France.

This Memorial bears the names of over 9,000 men who fell in the period from 8 August 1918 to the date of the Armistice on 11 November 1918 in the Advance to Victory in Picardy and Artois between the Somme and Loos and who have no known grave.

Fred Trim was awarded The British War and Victory Medals.

VIS-EN-ARTOIS BRITISH CEMETERY
and the
VIS-EN-ARTOIS MEMORIAL
Haucourt Pas de Calais France

Arthur Frederick Dommett was born in Dalwood in 1890. He was baptised at St. Peter's Church on 16 August 1891. The 1891 census return records Arthur Dommett was aged 11 months and the youngest child of John George and Elizabeth Dommett and they were living in a four room dwelling in Dickens Marsh Dalwood. His parents were both born in Shute and his father was a Carpenter. He had two sisters and three brothers.

In 1901 Arthur Dommett aged 10 was now living with his parents back in Whitford. His father George 57 a working Carpenter and his mother was a Needlewoman making shirts at home and also living there was his sisters Sarah aged 25 a Domestic servant and Mabel 18 and brothers William 20 born in Shute and Henry 16 and Ephraim 13 born in Dalwood.

In 1911 Arthur Dommett was working as a Labourer and living back at Dickens Marsh in Dalwood with Elizabeth Carter 93 and her daughter 48 in a three room dwelling which was next door to the four room dwelling where his parents were now also living back in Dalwood. Arthur Frederick Dommett first entered service in France on 25 July 1915 as Private No. 10048 in the Devonshire Regiment.

Private ARTHUR FREDERICK DOMMETT No. 16016 of the Dorsetshire Regiment 2nd Battalion (formerly No. 10048, Devonshire Regiment) died of wounds incurred on 1 May 1916 age 25 fighting in the Gallipoli Campaign. He is Remembered with Honour at the Amara War Cemetery Iraq then known as Mesopotamia which contains 4,621 burials of the First World War.

Arthur Frederick Dommett was awarded three Medals for his war service – The Star, and Victory Medals.

7. The Men Born in Dalwood not named on the Dalwood Memorial who Died in the Great War

The names of two men born in Dalwood who died in the Great War were not included on the Dalwood War Memorial as they had connections with other parishes.

William James Glade born in Dalwood Remembered in Stockland. Private No. 14883 the Devonshire Regiment 9th Battalion was killed in action in France and Flanders on 1 July 1916.

William James Glade was born in Dalwood in 1882 the son of George and Mary Ann Glade. In 1891 the family was living at Hawley Bottom in Dalwood where his father George Glade was 51 a Farmer of eight acres with his wife Mary Ann aged 50 and William 9. William Glade attended Dalwood School from 14/3/1887 to 11/3/1895. In 1901 William Glade aged 19 years an Agricultural Labourer was living at the Royal Oak Inn in Stockland and in Cotleigh Devon with his uncle Publican Joseph Hane 66 and his wife Elizabeth 70 and sister Evelina 24. In 1911 William Glade Farm Labourer was living in Cotleigh Devon boarding with J. G. Stamp and his wife.

William Glade's name is on the Stockland War Memorial.

––––––––

Lisle Frank Loveridge Private No. 2558 of the 1st/4th Bn., Devonshire Regiment who died age 23 on 3 July 1916 in Mesopotamia in the Gallipoli Campaign. He was born in Dalwood and is Remembered in Kilmington.

Lisle Frank Loveridge's photograph is included in Azulay Wallace's collage of Dalwood's *Fallen Heroes*. Lisle Loveridge was born in

Dalwood at Woodhayes Farm. He was born on 5 March 1893 and was baptised at St. Peter's Church Dalwood on 2 April 1893 as Lisle Frank Loveridge the son of Henry and Minnie Loveridge. He attended Dalwood Board School from 25/4/1893 to 24/3/1899 when the family moved to Dulcis Farm Kilmington where they were recorded living in the 1901 census returns. His parents later moved to Shiphay Farm Colyton, Devon.

Lisle Frank Loveridge's name is on the Kilmington War Memorial.

Part Two

Dalwood Men Who Served in The Great War 1914-1919

8. Military Records for other Dalwood Men who Served in the Great War 1914-1919

This image shows the page in a Financial Account Book for the years 1917-1918 which lists names of men connected with the parish of Dalwood and surrounding areas in the parish of Stockland who enlisted and fought in the Great War. Some of them are the men who died but there are others for whom some military records have been found.

1914 – 1918 Dalwood War List

The Financial Account Book records the efforts of local Dalwood parishioners to raise money to send out gifts in the form of Postal Orders to men on Active Service at Christmas time in the years 1917 and 1918. In November 1917 a Dalwood Whist Drive Committee raised a total of £7 16s. 8d. A Receipt for the purchase of Postal Orders – one Postal Order at 10s. and thirty nine at 5/- plus Stamps at 3s. 3d. was given by B.P. Cox of the Post Office Stores Dalwood. In 1918 a Collection is recorded for Christmas Gifts for Dalwood Men on Active Service this year in place of holding Whist Drives or an Entertainment which raised the sum of £12. There is a record of payment made to B.P. Cox of the Post Office Stores for 33 Postal Orders at 6 shillings five cash payments at 6 shillings each 33 stamps and Envelopes and Paper. It seems holding Whist Drives to raise money for Christmas during this war started in Dalwood in 1915. In December 1915 there is a report of a Whist Drive for Servicemen held in *The Western Times* dated 3 December 1915:

Dalwood: A Whist Drive was held by the kind permission of the Managers in the Schoolroom on Friday and was very well attended. The proceeds after paying expenses will be used in providing Christmas comforts for our brave Dalwood men serving in the Army or Navy. All the games were keenly contested and the prizes were won by: – Ladies: 1 Mrs Edwards 2 Mrs Broom Booby prize: Miss Turner. Gentlemen: 1 Mr C. Trim 2 Mr F. Spiller Booby Mr A. White. The prizes were kindly given by Mesdames Bromfield Parrett Edwards and Mr Hammett. At the conclusion of the games Mr Bennett thanked all present for their attendance and for supporting such a worthy cause...A vote of thanks to the Committee for providing a pleasant evening was given. Over £8 has been made by the two Whist Drives. The singing of the National Anthem brought an enjoyable evening to a close.

Records for these Men from Dalwood and the surrounding area show they enlisted over the period from 1915-1917.

At the outbreak of war in 1914 the government relied on volunteers to join the regular army – they had to pass a medical test and mostly had a choice which regiment to join. By the Spring of 1915 it had become clear that voluntary recruitment was not going to provide the numbers of men required. The Government passed the National Registration Act on 15 July 1915 to assess numbers and occupations. In 1916 enlistment was made compulsory when the Government introduced the Military Service Act on 27 January 1916. All British males were now deemed to have enlisted – that is they were conscripted if they were aged between 18 and 41 years and resided in Great Britain (excluding Ireland) and were unmarried or a widower on 2 November 1915. This act was extended to married men on 25 May 1916. More than 2.3 million conscripts were enlisted before the end of the war in November 1918.

A system of local Appeals Tribunals was established to hear cases of men who believed they were disqualified on the grounds of ill-health occupation or conscientious objection. Some trades were deemed to be vital to the war economy: they were called *starred occupations*. Several Dalwood men appeared before the Axminster Tribunals. Conscription ceased on 11 November 1918 and all conscripts were discharged if they had not already been so on 31 March 1920.

The British Soldier's Individual Military Service Records – records for some individuals can be found but unfortunately many of these Military Records were destroyed or damaged by a fire the result of enemy bombing in 1940. Hence many records have not been found. The Military Records consisted of the following:

1. Attestation Form stating the date and terms on which a man joined up with the following Questions to be put to the Recruit before Enlistment: Name and Address Whether British Subject Age Trade or Calling Single or Married Whether in Majesty's Forces Previously Willing to be Vaccinated Did you receive a Notice and do you understand its meeting and who gave it to you... An Oath to be Taken by Recruit on Attestation swearing an oath of allegiance to George V recorded with a witness...Certificate signed by Magistrate or Attesting Officer...

2. Records of Postings and Transfers are the events of the soldier's time in the army on a Military History Sheet Medical History and Casualty and Return to Active Service.

3. The Discharge at the end of the soldier's time in the army is recorded in a Discharge Certificate and Transfer to Reserve.

4. Campaign Medals Index An Index of Medals awarded to men who qualified by taking part in the World War 1 was kept.

5. Records for Men who Emigrated – Five Dalwood men who fought in the War are known to have emigrated before the start of the War in 1914. Some of their emigration records have been found on www.shipspassengersonline.

John Beard of Ham Farm Stockland Devon

John Beard was born 13 November 1892 at Ham Farm in Ham in the parish of Stockland the only son of Frederick and Sarah Beard. He was baptised 11 December 1892 at St. Peter's Church Dalwood. John Beard was admitted to Dalwood Board School on 5/7/1897 and remained a pupil there until 16/11/1906 when he left to work on his parent's farm. In 1901 John Beard aged 8 was living with his parents at Ham Farm. Ten years later he is recorded in the 1911 census as 18 years of age a Farmer's son living with parents Frederick Beard aged 42 and Sarah 44.

John Beard Private No. 87478 in the Devonshire Royal Regiment of Artillery Military Records

John Beard enlisted on 25 May 1915 aged 23 years at Axminster Devon when he was enrolled as Private No. 87478 in the Devonshire Royal Regiment of Artillery. He gave his next of kin as his father Frederick Beard of Ham Farm Stockland. He first served at Home with 3rd Devonshire Royal Field Artillery No. 8 District. From June 1915 he served as a Driver in the BEF in France and Belgium. On 11 July 1919 John Beard was discharged to the address Millhayes Mills in Stockland Devon.

John Beard's military records contain a copy of a letter to the Officer in Charge from his father Fred written 29 July 1916 with address Ham Farm enquiring about his son's whereabouts:

Dear Sir Will you kindly send me any information you can give of my son Driver John Beard 87478 HQS 20th DAC Force Belgium As we have not heard anything for over 2 months and he is the only one His Mother is much worried about it Any news you can send we will be very grateful Truly F. Beard.

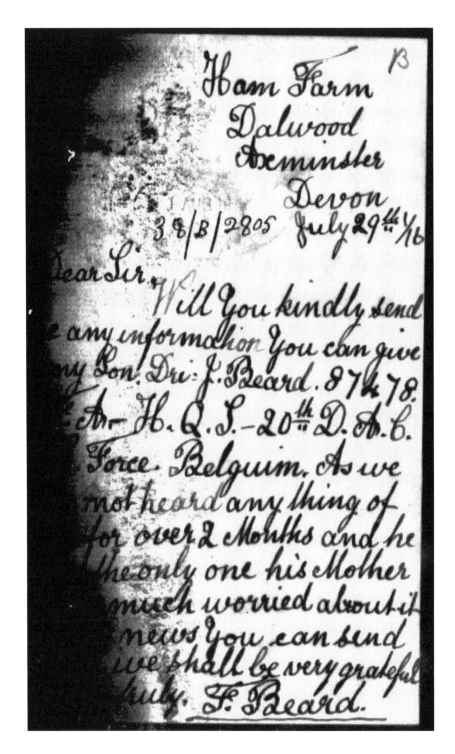

B

Ham Farm
Dalwood
Axminster
Devon
3 8/3/2805 July 29th /16

Dear Sir,

Will you kindly send me any information you can give my Son. Dri: J. Beard. 87478. Ar H.Q.S.—20th D.A.C. Force. Belguim. As we not heard any thing of for over 2 Months and he he only one his Mother much worried about it news you can send we shall be very grateful truly. F. Beard.

Arthur Eli Cleall of Ridge Cottages Stockland Devon

Arthur Eli Cleall was born 8 December 1887 the youngest son of Eli and Hannah Cleall of Ridge Cottages near Ham in the parish of Stockland. In 1891 3 year old Arthur was living with his parents Eli Cleall 41 Farm labourer and Hannah 42 and sisters Alma 12 Julia 9 and Lily 5. Arthur Cleall was admitted to Dalwood Board School on 4/7/1892 and left 31/1/1902. In 1901 Arthur now aged 13 was still living at Ridge Cottage Ham with his father Eli Cleall 51 a Horse Carter and mother Hannah 52. In 1913 his father Eli Cleall was awarded a Prize for Long Service for Men over 40 years with Mr Nicholas Pomeroy of Ridge Farm Stockland where the Annual Ploughing Match between Stockland Dalwood and Membury was being held that year.

Ridge Cottages near Ham in Stockland

Arthur Eli Cleall Private No. 153890 Machine Gun Corps Military Records

On 15 February 1916 Arthur Eli Cleall aged 28 years 2 months enlisted at Honiton Devon. He gave his occupation as a Carter. He was first enrolled as a Private in the Queen's Own Royal West Kent Regiment and later transferred to the Machine Gun Corps. On 3 September 1919 he was declared *Unfit for Service* and admitted to Hospital. There are records for him at Crediton and Exeter hospitals for treatment to a serious injury to his left arm. Arthur Cleall was awarded The British War and Victory Medals.

Arthur's parents Eli and Hannah Cleall of Ridge Cottage Stockland were buried in Dalwood Churchyard Hannah on 6 December 1927 aged 79 and Eli on 11 January 1928 aged 78. Their gravestone can be seen to the left of the main path. Their son Arthur Eli Cleall died in 1945.

Cecil Dening of Higher Way Dalwood Devon

Cecil James Dening was born in 1889 in the parish of Shute Devon where two generations of his family were farmers at Pacehayne Farm – his grandfather Cleophas Dening and his father Charles Dening. In 1891 Cecil's grandparents Cleophas Dening aged 63 Farmer and his wife Susan had come to live in the parish of Dalwood lodging at a Cottage in Andrewshayes Lane Dalwood. Ten years later in 1901 Cleophas Dening aged 72 born in Shute was listed as a Grocer living at Tucks Cottage in Dalwood with wife Susan 56 – this cottage is now known as The Retreat in Andrewshayes Lane.

In 1891 their grandson Cecil Dening aged 1 was living at Spillers Cottage Shute with his parents Charles Dening 29 an Agricultural labourer and Janie 26 and brother Hubert 3. By 1901 Cecil now aged 10 was living at Higher Way Farm on Dalwood Hill in the parish of Dalwood – his father Charles 38 still working as an Agricultural labourer mother Janie 37 and brothers Frank 13 and Leonard 10. In 1911 19 year old Cecil Dening was a Cycle Makers Assistant still living at Higher Way Dalwood with mother Janie 48 and one servant Susan Ellis.

Cecil Dening Private No. 17195 The Devonshire Regiment Military Records

On 19 February 1916 Cecil James Dening aged 25 years and 4 months a Grocery Deliverer enlisted in the army in Axminster Devon. He was recorded as Private No. 17195 serving in the Devonshire Regiment at Home until 14 May 1917 when he was transferred to the Labour Corps.

He served with the BEF in France from 3 December 1917 and was discharged in 1919. Cecil Dening was awarded The British War and Victory Medals.

After he was demobilised Cecil Dening returned to live and work in Dalwood. He married Ethel Sarah Spiller on 22 October 1927 at St. Peter's Church. She was the daughter of farmer Philip Spiller who farmed at Naishes Farm on Danes Hill. Cecil and Ethel lived at Hill View Cottages in the centre of the village. Cecil gave his occupation as a Motor Driver on the marriage certificate. He ran a Taxi business and kept two pumps selling petrol in a garage at the centre of the village opposite the Tucker's Arms.

Cecil and Ethel Dening with their Pumps in Dalwood

William Vessey Lavender of Penny Hill Farm Stockland Devon later of Walnut Cottage Dalwood

William Vessey Lavender was born in Islington London in 1887. In 1901 he was living at Penny Hill Farm in the parish of Stockland Devon with his father William Lavender 41 Farmer and mother Harriet 39. On 6 October 1909 he married Ethel Marsh Bromfield at St. Peter's Church Dalwood. She was the daughter of John Bromfield Farmer of Ridge Farm Stockland who later retired to live at Walnut Cottage Dalwood. Ethel's brother Percy J Bromfield also served in the Great War.

In 1911 William Vessey Lavender aged 24 was listed as the Farmer at Penny Hill Farm Stockland with his wife Ethel 28. On 7 May 1914 William V. Lavender aged 28 Farmer embarked from London on the ship *Osterley* of the Orient Line bound for Fremantle Western Australia.

William Lavender enlisted in Australia in 1916 with the Australian Imperial Forces for which the Australian National Archives have detailed records.

William V. Lavender Private No. 820 with the 34th Infantry Battalion Australian Imperial Forces Military Records

William V. Lavender enlisted as Private No. 820 with the 34th Infantry Battalion Australian Imperial Forces at West Maitland New South Wales Western Australia on 17 January 1916 aged 29 years and 11 months. He was then a Farm labourer and gave his next of kin as his wife Ethel Lavender of Walnut Cottage Dalwood Devon England. On 2 May 1916 William Lavender embarked with his unit from Sydney Australia on the *HMAT Hororata No. A20* disembarking on 23 June 1916 at Plymouth England.

After a period of training William Lavender proceeded overseas to serve in France on 21 November 1916. On 29 May 1917 William Lavender was reported as wounded in action on the Field and admitted to King George Military Hospital England on 5 June 1917.

Australian Imperial Force Attestation Paper for William Vessey Lavender Service Abroad Private No. 820 34 Battalion 17 January 1917

Born in London England aged 29 years and 11 months Farm Labourer Wife Ethel Lavender of Walnut Cottage Dalwood Axminster Devon.

Statement of Service for Private No. 820 W. V. Lavender

1916 24 November Proceeded overseas to France from Southampton.

1917 28 May Wounded in action on the Field.

1917 5 June Transferred to King George's Hospital in England.

1917 6 December Victoria Barracks Sydney Private No. 820 Lavender of 34th Battalion returned to Australia per *HMAT Ulysses*

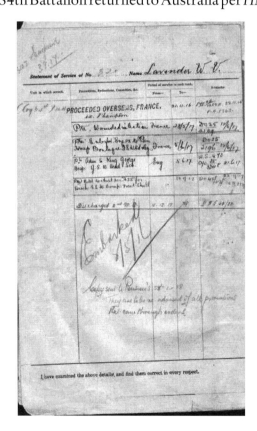

Statement of Service for Private No. 820 W. V. Lavender

on 16 November 1917 – Discharged from the Australian Imperial Force in consequence of *Medical Unfitness* on 15 December 1917. He was awarded The Star, British War and Victory Medals.

William Lavender had one son named as William John Bromfield Lavender. William Lavender died in Australia on 30 April 1968 and was buried at Smithfield Anglican Cemetery New South Wales Australia.

William Henry Wheaton of Higher Corrie Stockland Devon

William Henry Wheaton or Bill as he was known was born in 1899 in Chard in Somerset the son of John and Ann Wheaton. In 1901 2 year old William Henry was living at Wellacombe in Chard with father John Wheaton aged 37 Dairyman and mother Ann 37 and sisters Ethel 10 and Rose 4. The 1911 census shows the family living at Shand Dairy Donyatt near Ilminster in Somerset. William Henry was now 12 years of age and still at school. The family later moved to farm at Higher Corrie Farm in the parish of Stockland.

William Henry Wheaton Private No. 58681 serving with King's Royal Rifle Corps Dorset Regiment Military Records

William Henry Wheaton enlisted on 21 December 1916 giving his age as 17 years old although still only 16. He gave his profession as a Wheelwright and his next of kin as his father John Wheaton of Higher Corrie Farm Stockland. He served on the Home Front until he was sent to join the BEF in France in March 1918. Here he was gassed and received a shell wound on 26 June 1918 and was transferred back to England. He was demobilised on 19 February 1919. He was awarded The British War and Victory Medals.

Bill Wheaton now returned home to work with his father at Higher Corrie Farm. Later he took an apprenticeship as a Cabinet maker in Yeovil Somerset. In 1923 William Henry Wheaton married Elsie May Summers daughter of Edmund and Rosa Summers in Upottery Devon. Following their marriage the couple moved to a smallholding in Stockland. Their only daughter Gwendoline Joy Wheaton was born here in 1925.

In 1931 the family moved to the parish of Dalwood to live at The Mill House by the River Corry with about twelve acres of land – The adjacent Dalwood Mill was burned down in 1909. His brother Fred Wheaton who had been living here with his family had moved to farm at Lower Lea Farm Dalwood.

Bill and Elsie May Wheaton's daughter Gwendoline Joy Wheaton married Arthur Raymond Quick at St. Peter's Church

The Mill House Dalwood

Bill Wheaton at The Mill Dalwood

Dalwood on 29 March 1948. Raymond's family were farmers at Rugg Farm Kilmington Devon. Raymond Quick recalls that Bill Wheaton kept several dairy cows. He used to wheel his churns from the Mill on the footbridge over the River Corry and along to the crossroads at the end of Lower Lane where he had built a milk stand for the daily collection by lorry.

Bill Wheaton was a skilled carpenter. He was a member of Dalwood Home Guard in the 2nd World War. From 1943 to 1963 Bill Wheaton was employed as the Sexton of St. Peter's Church Dalwood – his wife Elsie was the Church Caretaker.

1973 Bill and Elsie Wheaton Celebrate their Golden Anniversary

Bill and Elsie Wheaton retired to Waggs Plot Axminster where Bill Wheaton died on 6 December 1989 aged 90 and his wife Elsie died in 1994 aged 94. Their ashes were buried in Dalwood Churchyard where there is a small memorial plaque to the left of the main Church door.

Charles John Perry of Harrisons Farm Stockland Devon

Charles John Perry known as John to the family was born in the parish of Luppitt Devon in 1898 the only son of Samuel and Annie Perry. In 1901 he was living at Budgels in Luppitt with his parents Samuel Perry aged 30 and Annie. By 1911 the family had moved to the Parish of Stockland where they were living at Harrisons Farm in Ham – Samuel Perry aged 40 was a Tenant farmer with his wife Annie 38 and son Charles John aged 12. John's son Gordon Perry recalls that his father attended a private school at Oaklands House in Dalwood run by the owner Miss Walker. This was the first house on the left down Marsh Lane below Carters Farm – now known as Whitegates.

Charles John Perry Private No. 28426 Hampshire Regiment Military Records

Charles John Perry was called up and enlisted at Axminster Devon on 14 May 1917 giving his address as Harrisons Farm Dalwood and his age as 18 years and 4 months working as a Farmer. He served on the Home Front until 1918 when he was posted to the BEF in France. He served in France from 29 January 1918 to 13 May 1918 when he was wounded in the arm. He was discharged *Unfit for War Service* on 20 February 1919. He had served two years and nine months.

After the War ended John Perry returned to work at Harrison Farm in Stockland which his father bought in 1920 together with the nearby Threshing Machine Cottage. He married Elizabeth Mary Chick in 1924. The couple first lived at Threshing Cottage in Ham where their daughter Goldye Perry was born in 1925 and then at Myrtle Cottage in Ham where their son Gordon Samuel John Perry was born in 1930.

John Perry took over Harrison Farm after the death of his father Samuel in 1936. John and Mary Perry retired from farming about 1960 when they swapped houses with their son Gordon and his wife Iris and moved to the bungalow named Bobhayes opposite Sunnylands Farm in Dalwood.

Mary Perry died in 1976 aged 79 and was buried in Dalwood Churchyard on 24 January 1976. John Perry died in 1988 aged 89 years – he was buried on 14 September 1988 with his wife.

Harrison Farm Ham in the Parish of Stockland

Frederick Mitchell Culverwell of Palmers Cottage Dalwood Devon

Frederick Mitchell Culverwell was born in Dalwood Devon on 25 June 1889 and baptised on 21 July 1889 at St. Peter's Church the son of William James and Ellen Culverwell. The Culverwell family was a family of Carpenters and Wheelwrights going back several generations in the parish of Dalwood. His father W. James Culverwell Carpenter had a Sawpit in the village centre by the Old Ford over the River Corry. He was Churchwarden of St. Peter's Church for 30 years – he made the coffins. There is a memorial plaque for him on the north wall inside the Church. He married Ellen Mitchell the daughter of the Landlord of the Tucker's Arms at St. Peter's Church on 5 April 1882.

In 1891 the family was living in Dalwood Village William J. Culverwell 31 Carpenter and wife Ellen 32 and three children Ida 7 Olive 6 and Fred aged 1 all born in Dalwood. Fred Culverwell was admitted to Dalwood Board School on 6/3/1893 and left 23/12/1903. In 1901 Frederick aged 11 was living in Dalwood Village at Palmers with parents W. James 41 Carpenter and Builder Ellen 42 and sisters Ida 17 Olive 16 Lois 9 and Jane 7. In 1911 Fred Mitchell Culverwell aged 21 was now listed working as a Furniture Salesman in Bournemouth Dorset lodging with F. J. Okey Draper. On 13 February 1913 Frederick Culverwell Salesman aged 22 emigrated to Australia embarking on board the ship *Orama* from London to Fremantle Western Australia.

Frederick M. Culverwell Private No. 2478 AIF Australian Imperial Forces Military Records

Frederick Culverwell enlisted in the Australian Imperial Forces on 6 May 1915 at the age of 24 years at Blackboy Hill Western Australia. He served as Private No. 2478 in the 11th Battalion 7th Reinforcement AIF. He gave his occupation as a Tree Feller who had worked for three years as an apprentice in the trade in Axminster Devon. His next of kin was his father William James Culverwell Dalwood Devonshire England.

On 25 June 1915 Fred Culverwell embarked with his unit from Fremantle Western Australia on board *HMAT A36 Karoola* for active service at the start of the Gallipoli Campaign.

Statement of Service of No. 2478 Frederick Mitchell Culverwell 1915-1917

After this campaign ended he was sent to France where on 1 March 1916 he disembarked in Marseilles. Two promotions followed – to Lance Corporal on 2 August 1916 and to Corporal on 25 September 1916. On 5 October 1916 he was seconded for Duty with the No.4 Officer Cadet Battalion training at Balliol College Oxford England. On 25 January 1917 he was promoted 2nd Lt. and on 13 February 1917 he proceeded overseas to France.

On 11 April 1917 2nd Lt. Frederick Culverwell was listed as Missing in Action and then reported as a Prisoner of War in Germany at Reincourt and interned at Munster No.1 Karlsruhe for the rest of the War. He was repatriated and returned to England on 1 January 1919. On 28 February 1919 he returned to Australia on the *SS Anchises* disembarking in Albany on 17 April 1919.

Fred Culverwell gave details of his service in World War 1 when he wrote the following letter to the Secretary Department of the Australian Army applying for the Anzac Medal and Badge which was to be awarded in 1967 to the surviving members of the Australian Forces who served in the Gallipoli Campaign to the final evacuation in January 1916:

Landed on Gallipoli with 6th and 7th Reinforcements of 11th Battalion AIF prior to and remained with unit until evacuated. Transferred to 51st Battalion in formation of 13th Brigade and served with this unit through the Somme Battle on the Western Front. Commissioned and posted to 16th Battalion in January 1917 and taken Prisoner of War at Bullecourt on 11 April 1917. Yours faithfully No. 2478 Frederick Mitchell Culverwell 11th 51st and 16th Battalion.

Fred Culverwell was awarded The Star, British War and Victory Medals.

Lt. Culverwell's return visit to his native village Dalwood in January 1919 was reported in the *The Western Times* 24 January 1919:

Lieut. F. M. Culverwell. A.I.F. of this village has just returned from Germany. At the outbreak war he joined up in Australia, and was sent to Gallipoli where he was wounded. After recovery he was sent to

France where he was again wounded and taken prisoner at Riencourt April 11 1917. During his captivity he was interned at Karlruhe Crefeld Strohen Moor and Bad Colberg. On his return to his native village the ringers welcomed him with a merry Peal.

Fred Culverwell returned to Perth Western Australia and was discharged from the AIF on 3 June 1919. He married Lillian Louisa Lockard in 1921. He is recorded in the Australian Electoral Rolls working as a Postmaster from 1937 at Reid New South Wales Australia. From 1958 he was at Woy Woy Robertson New South Wales Australia. He died there on 29 June 1976 aged 87.

Edward Trim of Eastons Cottage Dalwood Devon

Edward Trim was born in 1884 in Musbury Devon the youngest son of George and Maria Trim. By 1891 the family was living in the parish of Dalwood at The Carpenters Arms – now a private house named Carpenters – where George Trim was the Innkeeper with wife Maria and children William 21 Thatcher George 19 Carpenter and Elizabeth 17 Maria 14 and Edward aged 11 years.

Ten years later in 1901 Maria Trim 63 now a widow and head of the household was listed as the Farmer at Burrough Farm Dalwood with her son Edward 21 an Agricultural labourer. Edward Trim married Elizabeth Partridge daughter of James Partridge Labourer on 12 December 1906 at St. Peter's Church Dalwood.

In 1911 Edward Trim aged 33 Farm Labourer was living at Eastons Dalwood with wife his wife Elizabeth 41 and daughter Madeline Trim aged 3 baptised at St. Peter's Church Dalwood on 27 September 1907.

Edward Trim Private No. 5228 'A' Company 4th Battalion Devon Regiment later Private No. 656 Agricultural Company in the Labour Corps Military Records

Edward Trim Agricultural labourer of Hawley Bottom Dalwood Devon was called up and enlisted on 1 June 1916 at Axminster Devon at the age of 37 years 11 months.

He had already served five years in the 3rd Devon Volunteers. He joined 'A' Company 4th Battalion Devon Regiment Reserve on 13 July 1916. His next of kin was his wife Elizabeth Trim of Hawley Bottom. He was mobilised on 17 August 1916 to serve on the Home Front. On 30 November 1917 he was transferred to serve as Private No. 656 Agricultural Company in the Labour Corps and continued to serve on the Home Front. He was demobilized on 26 March 1919 giving his address as Hawley Bottom Dalwood Devon.

1916 13 July Axminster Attestation of No. 5228 Edward Trim 4th Devon Regiment

The Davey Family Military Records

As we have seen there are four Davey names inscribed on the Dalwood Great War Memorial who died on the Western Front in France and Flanders. Seven other members of this Davey family fought in the Great War – John, Harry, James, Robert, William, Arthur and Fred.

The following Military Service records have been found:

The two Sons of Albion and Sarah Davey of Hawley Bottom Dalwood – Walter and James

Walter Davey their youngest son baptised 1882 20 August at St. Peter's Church killed in action on 26th September 1917.

James Davey born 11 June 1879 and baptised at St. Peter's Church on 1 July 1879. In 1881 the family was living at No. 1 Ham Cottage in the parish of Stockland father Albion 40 an Agricultural labourer with Sarah Anne 40 and children John 11 Susan 7 born in Cheshire and Frances 5 and James 2 born in Dalwood. James Davey was admitted to Dalwood Board School on 7/5/1883 and left in 1893. James Davey is recorded as living with his family in Hawley Bottom in the census returns of 1891 and in 1901 when James Davey aged 20 was a recorded as a Cowman.

Private James Davey No. 7607 in The Devonshire Regiment Military Records

James Davey first enlisted in the army at Exeter Devon in January 1904 and joined the Devonshire Regiment at the age of 23 years 10 months. He served at Home for one year and 20 days until 16 February 1905. He then served in India for two years and 39 days from 17 February 1905 to 27 March 1907. He was then transferred to the Army Reserve serving at Home for seven years and 136 days.

James Davey married Beatrice Lily Barratt on 1 August 1909 at St. Mary's Church Axminster Devon. In the 1911 census James Davey aged 29 was listed as a Grocer and Corn Merchant living at No. 3 Cottage Lyme Rd. Axminster Devon with wife Beatrice Lily White 23 and son Cecil James 10 months old. At the start of the War James Davey was mobilized on 5 August 1914 at Exeter Devon and served in France for three years and 105 days until 3 December 1917 when he was transferred to the Labour Corps. He was demobilised at Nottingham on 2 March 1919 when he was described as of *Very Good Character.*

Four sons of Thomas and Hannah Davey of Hawley Bottom Dalwood born and baptised in Dalwood served in the Great War.

1882 Tom Davey emigrated to America in 1913. See below for further information.
1891 John Davey emigrated to Australia died in the war. As previously described in Part One of this book.
1896 Fred Davey for whom no military records found.
1897 Arthur Davey. See below for further information.

Tom Davey born 11 June 1882 was baptised on 2 July 1882 at St. Peter's Dalwood the son of Thomas and Hannah Davey Labourer. In 1891 Tom aged 8 was living with his family in Hawley Bottom Thomas Davey 44 Gardener Hannah 35 Walter 12 Sarah 4 Annie 2 and Lodger John K Fry 39 Carpenter. Tom Davey was admitted to Dalwood Board School 8/5/1888 and left 22/3/1895. In 1901 Tom Davey now aged 18 was a Coach Builder still living with his family in Hawley Bottom Dalwood. In 1911 Tom Davey 28 Carpenter and Wheelwright was living in Ilton Somerset with his elder brother Charles Davey aged 31 Carpenter and Wheelwright and his wife Lavinia 32 and their children Ronald 6 and Ada 1. His younger brother Fred Davey Wheelwright learning the Business born Dalwood was also living here.
    1913 Tom Davey aged 31 emigrated to America embarking for New York from the port of Queenstown County Cork Ireland on 30 March on the ship *Franconia* of the Cunard Line. On 6 April 1917 America entered the War declaring war on Germany. All

males had to register with the WW1 American Draft Registration Cards.

1917 12 September Tom Davey was Registered No. 3460 in the WW1 American Draft Registration Cards aged 35 years working as a miner for the Prime Exploration Company of Denver Colorado. He gave his next of kin as Mrs Elizabeth Davey of Cleaton Cumberland England. No more records have been found for Tom Davey.

Arthur Davey was the youngest of the four brothers born in Dalwood who fought in the Great War. Arthur Davey was born 16 September 1897 and baptised on 5 December 1897 at St. Peter's Dalwood son of Thomas and Hannah Davey. In 1901 Arthur aged 3 was living in Hawley Bottom Dalwood with his family Thomas Davey 54 Groom and General Gardener Hannah 46 and elder brothers and sisters George 24 Railway Plate Layer Walter 22 Miller's Labourer Tom 18 Coach builder Annie 12 John 9 Euphemia 6 and Fred 5 all born in Dalwood. Arthur Davey was admitted to Dalwood Board School on 19/5/1903. In 1911 Arthur 13 a Scholar was still at Hawley Bottom with parents Thomas Davey 63 Farm labourer Hannah 57 and sister Euphemia 16 Domestic servant. He left Dalwood School on 18 September 1911 to work at Mr Adamsons.

Arthur Davey Private No. 28449 Devonshire Regiment Military Records

Arthur Davey of Hawley Bottom Dalwood a Cowman aged 18 years and 2 months enlisted on 22 November 1915 at Axminster Devon and was posted to the Devonshire Regiment Army Reserve in Agricultural employment. He was mobilised from the Reserve to fight on 15 July 1916. On 11 December 1916 he was relegated to the Reserve *for as long as it is necessary to retain him in Agricultural employment*. He was later discharged having suffered an injury – the date of his discharge is not known.

1922 On 26 April 1922 Arthur Davey aged 24 Farm Worker of Blamphayne Farm Northleigh Devon emigrated to Australia embarking from London to Melbourne on the *Beltana*. On 20 November 1939 he married Ethel Dorothy Stephens at Beeac Victoria Australia. Arthur Davey died on 3 January 1987 in Victoria Australia. Thomas and Hannah Davey emigrated from Dalwood to America where they are recorded in the census of 1920 living in Denver Colorado.

* * * * * * *

Three sons of Emanuel Davey Railway Plate Layer and Mary Ann Davey of Hawley Bottom Dalwood fought in the Great War.

Harry Davey the eldest son baptised 1 August 1880 at St. Peter's Church Dalwood is named as a Soldier living in Ham Stockland with his wife Clara Elizabeth on the baptism register of his two daughters Mabel Mary baptised 15 November 1914 at St. Peter's Church and Ethel Dorothy baptised 14 July 1918. No surviving military records have been found for Harry Davey.

Robert Emanuel Davey Davey baptised 7 October 1894 - no military records found.

Michael Davey born 1898 died on 8 October 1918 as recorded in Part One.

* * * * * * *

James and Mary Ann Davey had eight children born in Hawley Bottom Dalwood. Their three sons fought in the Great War.

William Davey was baptised 27 August 1882. No military records have been found but he is mentioned in his brother John's Enlistment details as being in the 1st Devons.

John Davey baptised 8 June 1884 – he enlisted in 1902. See records below.

Charles Davey born in 1897 was killed in action as recorded in Part One of this book.

John Davey was born in Ham Stockland and baptised on 8 June 1884 at St. Peter's Church Dalwood son of James and Mary Ann Davey of Battle Cottage Hawley Bottom. In 1891 John aged 6 was living at Hawley Bottom Dalwood with his family James Davey 37 Agricultural Labourer Mary Ann 34 and William 8 Sarah 5 Florence 2 and Elizabeth 6 months. John Davey was admitted to Dalwood Board School on 7/4/1890 and left on 19/2/1897. Records for John Davey in the 1901 census have not been found.

On 24 July 1908 John Davey married Ellen Hawkins daughter of Edward Hawkins. In 1911 John Davey 26 General labourer was living at Myrtle Grove Hawley Bottom Dalwood with wife Ellen 24 and with daughter Evelyn aged 3 born in Ash Surrey.

Military Records for John Davey Driver No. 18914 in the Army Service Corps previously in the Devonshire Regiment

1902 John Davey of Stockland aged 18 years Labourer son of James Davey enlisted in the Army Service Corps on 18 January 1902 at Axminster Devon. Prior to this he had belonged to the 4th Devonshire Regiment in which he was still serving.

1904 30 December Driver John Davey No. 18914 had served 2 years 11 months. He re-engaged for a further 8 years saying the he was willing to serve abroad. He served in the 4th Devonshire Regiment at Home as a Driver until 17 January 1914 a total of 12 years. At the age of 26 years he applied to remain in the Reserve. His conduct was recorded as 'Very Good.' He gave his address as Ridge Cottages Stockland Devon.

1913 On 11 December John Davey Driver No. 18914 re-engaged in the Army Reserve for four more years – he signed on in Reading Berkshire. John Davey served in France for three years 105 days from 21 August 1914 to 3 December 1917 and then at Home until the end of the War.

The Edwards Family Military Records

Three members of the family of William Edwards Junior Dalwood Shopkeeper and his wife Mary Ann served in the Army in the Great War. Their son Britton John Edwards was killed in action in 1918 as recorded in Part One of this book.

The Western Times on 5 July 1918: *News has been officially received that Private B. J. Edwards of the Devons is missing in France. He is the son of the late Mr W. Edwards and of Mrs Edwards f Danes Villa Dalwood. He was previous to his enlistment cashier in Lloyds Bank at Teignmouth. Mrs Edwards has two other sons serving one of whom Private V. H. Edwards is in hospital suffering from a compound fracture of the left arm. He was in Canada at the outbreak of the war and came over with the 5th Canadians. This is the third time he has been wounded. The other son is Trooper Allan D. Edwards who is serving in Palestine.*

Victor Harry Edwards was born 20 October 1886 and baptised 17 December 1886 at St. Peter's Church. He was admitted to Dalwood School 10/11/1890 and left 29/3/1901. In 1901 the Edwards family was at Danes Villa on Danes Hill in Dalwood – now named Danesfort – William Edwards Junior Retired Grocer 63 and wife Mary 47 and William 21 Victor 14 Ellen 12 and Allan Dymond aged 6 all born in Dalwood.

Victor Harry Edwards returned to fight in the Canadian Expeditionary Force after emigrating to Canada before the war. Information from Canadian National Archives is recorded:

EDWARDS, VICTOR HARRY Regimental number: 105405 Reference: RG 150, Accession 1992-93/166, Box 2846 – 32

Allan Dymond Edwards was born in Dalwood 12 August 1894. He was admitted to Dalwood Board School 5/2/1900 and left 1/5/1908.

In 1911 Allan Edwards 16 Auctioneers Clerk was at Danes Villa Dalwood with his father William 73 Retired Grocer and mother Mary Ann 58 and brother Ernest 26 Farmer and sister Ellen 22. No military records found have been found for him.

Names of Dalwood Men who fought in the Great War

No Military Records have been found at this time for the other thirty-six names of Dalwood men recorded as serving in the Armed Forces in the Church Financial Book 1917-1918:

Anning Ernest   no definite records found

Appleford William   his wife Elizabeth lived at Brook Cottage in Dalwood during the war – in 1917 daughter Winifred Marjorie was baptised at St. Peter's Church 8 April 1917

Bartlett Tom   no definite records found

Bazley Walter   no definite records found

Boyland Robert   no definite records found

Bromfield Percy J   1884 born Stockland son of John and Mary Bromfield Farmer

Cook Leonard   1884 born Feniton Devon son of George & Emily Hutchings Farm

Cook Reginald   1887 born Feniton Devon son of George & Emily Hutchings Farm

Cox Harry   no definite records found

Cox Fred   no definite records found

Davey Robert   7 October 1894 baptised Dalwood son of Emanuel and Mary Anne

Davey William   1882 born son of James and Mary Ann Davey Hawley Bottom

Davey Fred   1896 born son of Thomas and Hannah Battle Cottage Hawley Bottom

Davey Harry   1880 Born son of Emanuel and Mary Ann of Hawley Bottom

Down William   no definite records found

French George	1890 born son of George & Elizabeth Bishop Dickens Marsh Dalwood
Gear Charles	1884 born son of James and Elizabeth Gear living in Dalwood 1891 and 1901
Gould Samuel G	1891 born son of Jethro & Mary Anna Gould of Coombes Middle Farm
Gould Arthur John	1887 born son of William & Emily Gould
Haysom George	no definite records found
Hutchings John	no definite records found
Jones Reginald	no definite records found
Lee William	no definite records found
Lee Harry	no definite records found
Loveridge Jesse	1887 born son of John & Catherine Blacksmith Ham Stockland brother of Heber Loveridge who died
Parrett Leslie	1890 son of Thomas B M and Zoe Parrett elder brother of Colin Parrett who died
Peach James	no definite records found
Peach George	no definite records found
Pratt William	1897 born son of William and Emily Pratt
Spiller Stanley F	no definite records found
Stapleforth Frank	1894 born Dalwood son of William & Martha Stapleforth Cattle Dealer
Trim Harry	1896 born son of George and Ellen Trim of Holmes Knapp Dalwood brother of Frederick Trim who died
Turner Arthur	1889 born son of Albert and Sarah Turner Slate House Dalwood
Turner Victor	1893 born son of Albert and Sarah Turner brother of above
Vine Edward	no definite records found
Wood Stanley	no definite records found

Acknowledgements

Photographs and Memories: I would like to thank the many people who have lent their photographs of Dalwood and spent time talking to me about their memories of Dalwood Past People and Places over the last three years. More books will be published with the information given to me.

In particular for this book I would like to thank the families of Fred Hoare and Charles John Perry and to thank Raymond Quick for records and photographs of the Wheaton family. Thank you to Graham Little for transcribing the Parish Records. Thank you to Susan Drew, Tony Drew, Roy Heard and Rita Thomas for the Dalwood photographs in this book and to Pat Ayshford and Fritz Reed for the photographs of Ham and Ridge in Stockland Parish.

Thank you to Owain Morgan without whose help this book would not have been published.

Other sources:

Census Returns for Dalwood Parish every ten years from 1841 to 1911. Records from the National Archives.

Dalwood St. Peter's Parish Registers now in the Devon Record Office.

Dalwood Board School opened in 1875 – the Admission Register starts 1875 giving the pupils' dates of birth name of the father and dates of admission and the date the pupil left.

Newspaper Articles found in the British Library Newspaper Archives.

The Commonwealth War Graves Commission 1914-1918 Debt of Honour Register.

The UK Soldiers Died in Great War 1914-1918 Register of Military Records. In 1921 His Majesty's Stationery Office published on behalf of and by authority of the War Office the list of those who died during the Great War.

Ships Passenger Lists Transcript Details on Ancestry.co.uk and findmypast.com.

Records of Emigration of five Dalwood men who are known to have emigrated before the start of the war in 1914 to Australia Canada and the USA.

Records of the Australian Imperial Forces in the Australian National Archives.

Canadian Expeditionary Force Records in Canadian National Archives.

WW1 American Draft Registration Cards

British Army WWI Pension Records 1914-1920 This contains service records of non-commissioned officers and other ranks who were discharged from the Army and claimed disability pensions for service in WWI.

British Army WWI Medal Rolls Index Cards, 1914-1920 This contains the Medal Rolls Index or Medal Index Cards. Every soldier qualified for at least one campaign medal and if he served overseas usually two or three. Each award was given in specific circumstances either for service at particular places and times, or for particular acts of bravery.

1914 Star For service under fire in France and Belgium 5 August to 22 November 1914.

British War Medal 1914-1920 For service abroad including India 5 August 1914 to 11 November 1918 or 1919 to 1920 in Russia.

Victory Medal 1914-1919 For military and civilian personnel who served in a theatre of war.

Appendix Index for Dalwood Great War Memorial

AIF Australian Imperial Forces

Allies: the armies primarily of Britain France Russia and America.

Armistice: signed at 11 a.m. on 11 November 1918 – an agreed cease-fire in the war on the Western Front that proved to be the end of the war.

ANZAC's: force from Australia and New Zealand.

BEF British Expeditionary Force: the professional army of Britain that went to France in 1914. 100,000 soldiers were sent to France at the start of the war but the BEF had lost 50,000 men by December 1914.

Canadian Expeditionary Force: expecting a war in Europe, during the summer of 1914 the Canadian government asked for volunteers to join a Canadian Expeditionary Force (CEF).

Central Powers: Germany, Austria and Turkey

CWGC Commonwealth War Graves Commission: The Commonwealth War Graves Commission holds a register of the death of every member of the Armed Forces and Civilians from the United Kingdom Australia Canada India New Zealand and South Africa who died in the Great War of 1914-1918.

Gallipoli Campaign: The eight month campaign in Gallipoli in 1915 was fought by Commonwealth and French forces in an attempt to force Turkey out of the war to relieve the deadlock of the Western Front in France and Belgium, and to open a supply route to Russia through the Dardanelles and the Black Sea. About 480,000 Allied troops took part in the Gallipoli campaign. The British had 205,000 casualties 43,000 killed. The Helles Memorial serves the dual function of Commonwealth battle memorial for the whole Gallipoli campaign and place of commemoration for many of those Commonwealth servicemen who died there and have no known grave.

Treaty of Versailles: peace terms signed with Germany on 28 June 1919.

Western Front: name of the front line of trenches that ran through France and Belgium. The Schlieffen Plan was devised by Schlieffen of the Germany Army before the war. The plan was based on the belief that Russia would take six weeks to get her army ready. In this time Germany would attack France defeat her and then turn the full force of her army against the Russians. It failed. For three years as a result of trench warfare the line on the Western Front barely moved.

Index